HOW TO
KIDS ON TRACK

Hari Datt Sharma

V&S PUBLISHERS

Published by:

V&S PUBLISHERS

F-2/16, Ansari road, Daryaganj, New Delhi-110002
☎ 23240026, 23240027 • *Fax:* 011-23240028
Email: info@vspublishers.com • *Website:* www.vspublishers.com

Regional Office : Hyderabad
5-1-707/1, Brij Bhawan (Beside Central Bank of India Lane)
Bank Street, Koti, Hyderabad - 500 095
☎ 040-24737290
E-mail: vspublishershyd@gmail.com

Branch Office : Mumbai
Jaywant Industrial Estate, 1st Floor–108, Tardeo Road
Opposite Sobo Central Mall, Mumbai – 400 034
☎ 022-23510736
E-mail: vspublishersmum@gmail.com

Follow us on:

Preface

Raising well-balanced children is an art. The sincerity of parents in discharging their responsibility towards their children will reflect in the development of the latter. In other words, as parents sow, so shall they reap – in the form of well-balanced children. Proper upbringing demands active effort, concern, sensitivity, understanding and empathy on the part of parents.

It is impossible to write a perfect prescription to mould ourselves into caring and successful parents. However, there are some guidelines that parents may find quite useful. One must note that there are many variations in parents, as there are in children. Furthermore, when we talk of parents and couples, we are not dealing only with two people but also with the net result of their interaction with each other. Also, remember that there are some prerequisites for effective parenting, just as there are for most tasks.

Every child needs emotionally stable parents who are mature and love each other. In homes where there is only one parent, his/her task becomes very complex, as s/he must take on many additional tasks ordinarily handled by the other parent.

Parents need to demonstrate their love for their children not only by their actions but also by the kind of environment they create in their homes. A child develops a feeling of security and confidence when he knows that he is loved.

Parents need to develop some understanding of their child's personality, as his talents, interests and aspirations mature. With this understanding, they can assist the child in aiming more accurately towards his goals, thus helping him fulfil his objectives.

Through discipline, guidance and encouragement, parents provide opportunities for the healthy exploration of natural surroundings by the child. They foster curiosity in their children to help them realise their full potential. Children who are deprived of such opportunities tend to fear the unknown and the future.

Parents must encourage children to express their true feelings. Successful parents imbue their family with a sense of belonging and provide opportunities for democratic planning and social action.

Consideration of and help for individual and family problems must be provided readily. The test of the genuineness of a problem lies more with the intensity of feeling about it, than with the nature of the problem itself. There are times when the father's needs must be, at least temporarily, relegated to second place because of the needs of his child. Successful parents constantly seek better ways to do what they have to do without affecting their attention towards their children.

A child's maladjustment with society often results from a poor parent-child relationship, which in turn often stems from lack of correct understanding by parents about their children. An adverse upbringing and the contemporary family situation are two powerful factors of maladjustment.

This book provides useful tips to parents to help their children develop normally – physically, mentally, emotionally and academically. Ignorance by parents about their child's special emotional and other needs can spoil the whole life of a child.

The main purpose of this book is to provide you with the necessary information to make you successful parents. Morals are imbibed and not taught. As the parents sow, so shall their children reap.

—Hari Datt Sharma
Founder
Peace of Mind Mission
New Delhi

Ten Commandments for a
Child's **Behaviour Development**

1. *When children live with encouragement, they develop CONFIDENCE.*

2. *When children live with tolerance, they learn to be PATIENT.*

3. *When children live with criticism, they learn to CONDEMN.*

4. *When children live with ridicule, they learn to be SHY.*

5. *When children live with hostility, they learn to FIGHT.*

6. *When children live with praise, they learn to APPRECIATE.*

7. *When children live with shame, they learn to feel GUILTY.*

8. *When children live with security, they learn to have FAITH.*

9. *When children live with approval, they learn to LIKE themselves.*

10. *When children live with acceptance, they learn to find LOVE.*

Contents

1

Parental Behaviour that Plays Havoc with Children

Contemporary research findings in the biological and social sciences have greatly advanced our understanding of the causes of abnormal behaviour exhibited by humans. It is mainly due to faulty development, severe stress or a combination of both.

When any child imbibes criminal values, he may become a criminal due to his faulty development. Faulty development is primarily responsible for the signs of abnormal behaviour in humans. The type of adjustment we are able to develop with people around us at any time is a function of both our personality development and the level of stress we face. Anything that leads to either faulty development or increased stress may create trouble.

If an individual is able to cope effectively with stressful situations, anxiety is eliminated. But if the anxiety and stress continue, the individual typically resorts to various ego-defence mechanisms, such as denial and rationalisation. This may result in lowered integration and maladaptive behaviour. The process of self-defence leads to incongruence between reality and the individual's competence. One should always bear in mind that *faulty learning is the main cause of faulty behaviour*.

Let us now understand the Ten Evils that play havoc with children.

Evil No. 1

Overprotection and Restrictiveness

Excessive maternal protection is called *momism*. It involves smothering the child's growth. Overprotective mothers watch over their children constantly, protect them from the slightest risk, and overly clothe and medicate them. They take decisions on their child's behalf at every opportunity, not allowing them to think for themselves. Different parental motivations may lead to overprotection.

Overprotection can decrease the urge to explore and take risks. And to the overprotected children, other children and adults may seem like awesome, frightful figures.

When the child's desire to seek independence are thwarted, he becomes frustrated. This sows the seeds of aggression and hostility in the child-parent relationship.

The mother's anxiety about the world is readily transmitted to the child. This provides a fertile ground for phobias, as well as for physical illness, which may be unconsciously encouraged by the mother if she has hidden motives to keep the child at home with her.

Overprotection may also cause excessive shyness and, as adults, these children might not be able to express themselves properly and be unable to take decisions independently. Ultimately, it may result in the following symptoms: temper tantrums, anger spasms, failure in school, school phobia and the like. All these end up in imparting an inadequate personality to the child. Such children often reach adolescence and early adulthood feeling inadequate and threatened by a "dangerous" world.

Closely related to overprotectiveness is restrictiveness. Here the parents rigidly enforce restrictive rules and standards, giving the child little freedom for growing in his own way.

In a study, Becker (1964) concluded that while restrictiveness fosters well-controlled socialised behaviour, it also tends to nurture fear, dependency, submission, repressed hostility and some dulling of intellectual striving. Often, extreme behaviour on the part of an adolescent is a way of rebelling against severe restrictions.

Main Causes of Overprotection

1. When a boy is born after a succession of girls in a family.
2. When s/he is the only child.
3. When the death of a sibling occurs.
4. When the child is handicapped.
5. When the child happens to be adopted.
6. When the child is born after the parents are past their prime.
7. When there have been a series of miscarriages.
8. When either of the parents is no more.

Evil No. 2

Rejection – a Masked Deprivation

Parental rejection of the child, though unintentional, is shown in various ways. This could include physical neglect, denial of love and affection, lack of interest in the child's activities and achievements, harsh or inconsistent punishment, failure to spend time with the child, remaining busy in activities like kitty-parties and lack of respect for the child's rights and feelings as a person. It could also involve cruel and abusive treatment. Parental rejection may be partial or complete, passive or active, and subtle or overtly cruel. Keeping the child in a crèche can also be a form of rejection.

The effects of rejection manifest in the child in the form of excessive fear, shyness, aggressiveness, thumb-sucking, bed-wetting, depression, temper tantrums, lying, stealing, slow morality development, low self-esteem, a feeling of insecurity, loneliness and an inability to express and receive love. All these arise at the subconscious level and the child cannot prevent their manifestation in his behaviour or personality.

Parental rejection is a major reason why adolescents run away from home.

Causes of Rejection

It appears that a large number of parents who neglect their children have themselves been victims of parental rejection. Later, even children who face parental rejection don't accept their parents when the latter grow old. So, rejection is not a one-way behaviour. That is why lack of love has been referred to as a *communicable disease*.

A child may be neglected without being rejected. For instance, when parents are too busy with their work or career, they neglect children.

Evil No. 3

Over-permissiveness and Indulgence

Allowing too much freedom of behaviour to children is called *permissiveness*. And allowing a child to do or have whatever s/he wants is termed *indulgence*.

Sometimes one or both parents seem always ready to indulge their child's smallest whims. In doing so, they fail to inculcate a desirable standard of behaviour in him. When parents indulge their child too much, it is bad for the child's development.

Overindulged children are characteristically spoiled, selfish, inconsiderate and demanding.

It is found that high permissiveness and low

punishment at home are positively correlated with *anti-social and aggressive behaviour,* particularly during the middle and later childhood.

Rejected and emotionally deprived children often find it difficult to enter into warm interpersonal relationships. When indulged children do enter into such relationships, they try to exploit people for their own interests in the same way that they have learned to exploit their parents.

If made to yield to authority, such children often turn rebellious, since they have had their own way for long.

Overindulged children also tend to be impatient. They approach problems in an aggressive and demanding manner. They find it difficult to accept present frustrations in the interests of long-term goals. The fact that their important and pampered status at home does not hold true in the outside world comes as a rude shock for indulged children. Confusion and difficulties in adjustment may occur, when reality forces them to reassess their assumptions about themselves and the world.

Evil No. 4

Parental Over-expectations

Some parents place excessive pressure on their children to make them live up to unrealistically high standards. Such parents expect their wards to excel in school and other activities. In the case of children who have the capacity to perform exceptionally well, things may work out to the parents' satisfaction.

Even so, the child may be under such sustained pressure that little room is left for spontaneity or development as an independent person. Mainly, the child is unable to quite live up to parental expectations and demands. If he improves his grade from C to B, he may be asked why he did not get A. Even if he succeeds in getting the A grade, the next expectation is to get an A+!

The parents always tell the child that he could do even better if he works harder. But no matter how hard he tries, he seems to fail in the eyes of his parents and, ultimately, in his own eyes. This results in painful frustration and self-devaluation. As the child is unable to live up to his parents' high expectations, his efforts seldom get parental approval and appreciation. This tends to discourage the child from making more efforts. The child eventually feels – I can't do it anyway, so why try?

There is nothing wrong with parental expectation vis-à-vis children. They help the child aim for a goal, which is good for his development. But expectations and demands that are too high (or too low) or distorted and rigid, can be a major cause of the child's faulty development and maladjustment.

Evil No. 5

Faulty Discipline

Many parents still believe that if they spare the rod, they will spoil the child. This indicates that many parents lack general guidelines for the proper upbringing of their child. One day, they may punish the child, but the very next day, they ignore his follies or even reward him.

Over-permissiveness and lack of discipline tends to produce a spoiled, inconsiderate, aggressive child. On the other hand, harsh discipline may have a variety of harmful effects, including fear of and hatred for the punishing person, curbing of initiative or spontaneity and less friendly feelings towards others.

Combined with restrictiveness, severe discipline also tends to incite rebellion and socially deviant behaviour in children, as they grow older.

When the child commits some folly, if the parents resort to physical punishment instead of withdrawal of approval and privileges, it may result in an increase in aggressive behaviour. Similarly, inconsistent discipline makes it difficult for the child to imbibe stable values to guide his behaviour.

When the child is punished once but ignored or rewarded the next time for the same behaviour, he is at a loss to understand what behaviour is appropriate. Parents must realise this and make it clear to the child too, that *it is the child's behaviour that is disapproved of and not the child itself.* The child must know clearly what kind of behaviour is expected from him, and to make this happen, positive and consistent methods of discipline should be worked out.

Evil No. 6

Favouritism

This arises from a variety of causes, which are more or less similar to those resulting in overprotection. The main causes: **1.** If the child is better looking or more intelligent than the other sibling. **2.** If there has been a sequence of girls and, finally, the much-desired boy is born.

The favoured child will encounter the same problems described earlier for the overprotected child. On the other hand, the disfavoured child may feel resentment against the parents and, perhaps, even towards the favoured child, showing little affection for them.

Evil No. 7

Maternal Deprivation

When infants are deprived of maternal stimulation as a result of separation from the mother, e.g. she could be a working woman or due to lack of adequate mothering at home, faulty development is the natural outcome.

When the mother devotes little attention to the child and, in the process, neglects or rejects it, the effects of such masked deprivation may be devastating. Mothers who reject or punish infants may cause tense, cranky and negative behaviour even at that early age. In case of early and prolonged deprivation, the damage to the infant may be irreversible or only partially reversible. Mothers who are regularly away at kitty-parties or inflict separation on their infants due to other preoccupations, and those who keep their child in a crèche, should be careful.

Evil No. 8

Faulty Family Patterns

As the infant grows into childhood, he must master new skills, learn proper assumptions about himself and the world and exert inner control over his behaviour. During this period, the family unit remains the crucial guiding influence for the child's personality development. Faulty family patterns are a fertile source for unhealthy development and maladjustment.

Recent research has revealed that maladjustive behaviour shown by the child may be fostered by the general family environment, as well as by the child's relationship with one or both parents.

An inadequate family lacks the resources, physical or psychological, for meeting demands with which most families can satisfactorily cope. The inadequate family relies heavily on sustained outside assistance and support in resolving its problems. Such a situation may stem from immaturity, lack of education, mental retardation or other shortcomings of the parents. Such families cannot give their children the feeling of safety and security they need, or adequately guide them in the development of essential competencies.

A disturbed family atmosphere has a bad effect on the child

In some disturbed families, parents are always fighting to maintain their own equilibrium and are unable to give the child the much needed love and guidance. Parental conflict and general tension are unfortunate conditions for the growing child.

Children tend to observe and imitate the behaviour of their parents. The parents prove to be undesirable role models for the children when they go by faulty realities, possibilities and value assumptions. It has a bad effect on the child if the parents depend excessively on defence mechanism in dealing with their problems. Examples of defensive behaviour: they blame one another or others for their own mistakes, they lie and cheat, they refuse to face and deal realistically with family problems and there is a marked discrepancy between their proclaimed values and those reflected in their actual behaviour.

A parent who is emotionally disturbed, addicted to alcohol or drugs, or otherwise maladjusted serves as an undesirable role model for his child.

In some families, parents engage in behaviour that violates the norms and interests of society. Children in such families simply observe and imitate the undesirable behaviour and attitudes of their parents. They may also acquire negative behavioural traits, like dishonesty, deceit, etc.

Maladaptive behaviour is much higher among children and adolescents from disruptive homes. Disruptive families are incomplete, whether as a result of death, divorce, separation or some other circumstances. Divorce leads to feelings of insecurity, rejection and conflicting loyalties. The loss of the father is more traumatic for a son than for a daughter.

Undesirable parental models are an important cause why mental disorders, delinquency, crimes and other forms of maladaptive behaviour tend to run in families.

Evil No. 9

Failure in Communication

Parents who discourage their child from asking questions fail to foster in him the skill that is essential for healthy development of his personality. Some parents are too busy with their own concerns to listen to their children. Consequently, they are unable to understand the conflicts and pressures their offspring are facing. During a crisis, such parents often fail to give the desired support and assistance to their children.

Many parents may convey one message by their words and another through their behaviour. For example, a father may deplore lying and sermonise to his son, "Never tell a lie", while he himself is prone to lying at the slightest pretext!

It is also a damaging communication pattern when parents, due to any prejudice or misconception, contradict or undermine the child's statements and conclusions, and he is left confused and devalued as a person.

Evil No. 10

Early Psychic Trauma

Many people have had traumatic experiences that temporarily shattered their feelings of security, adequacy and worth. Such experiences later on play a major role in influencing their evaluation of themselves and the environment they live in. These traumas are bound to leave psychological wounds that never heal completely. That is why, one person feels quite stressed while facing a particular problem, while this is not at all stressful for the other person.

Early traumas seem to have more far-reaching consequences than later ones, because critical evaluation, reflection and self-defences are not yet well developed in children.

Ten Commandments for the Child's Behaviour Development

1. When children receive regular encouragement, they develop *confidence*.
2. When children are taught tolerance, they learn to be *patient*.
3. When children are exposed to criticism, they learn to *condemn*.

4. When children live amidst ridicule, they learn to be *shy*.

5. When children live amidst hostility, they learn to *fight*.

6. When children receive praise, they learn to *appreciate*.

7. When children live with shame, they learn to feel *guilty*.

8. When children live in security, they learn to have *faith*.

9. When children live with approval, they learn to *like* themselves.

10. When children live with acceptance, they learn to find *love*.

ooo

2

As Parents Sow, So the Children Reap

Family Circumstances Abetting Maladjustment

Within the family circle emotions run wild and deep. The home is in many ways a miniature world, for here are found the forces that shape personality, the feelings that will determine the quality and quantity of relationships a child will form with his peer group and, ultimately, with his intimate adult companions.

While it is true that during the school years the child becomes less homebound, nonetheless the influence of parents during this period is profound. The home establishes rules, ideas and values by which the child comes to measure life and those who share his life.

Given below is a brief description of the families where children are prone to acquire negative behavioural traits:

1. **Antisocial Families:** In these families, parents are overtly or covertly engaged in behaviour that violates the norms and interests of society. Children in such families may be taught or may themselves emulate acts of dishonesty, deceit and other undesirable behaviours and attitudes of their parents.

2. **Disturbed Families:** In disturbed families, children are prone to psychological disorders. Here, parents with grossly eccentric and

abnormal personalities may keep the home in constant emotional turmoil.

3. **Inadequate Families:** Such families are unable to cope with ordinary problems of family living due to lack of resources. These families cannot give their children the required feeling of safety and security. Also, they cannot adequately guide and encourage their children to develop skills that are essential to succeed in life.

4. **Disrupted Families:** These families come into being as a result of the death of a parent, due to divorce or separation or some other circumstances. Children of these families suffer from insecurity and rejection complex.

5. **Mother Threatens to Desert:** In some families, the mother often threatens to desert or sometimes actually deserts the family for short periods. In such families, the child is likely to show mother-anxiety symptoms. Often, the child will develop hostility towards the mother.

6. **Deep Estrangement Between Parents:** In a family where deep estrangement prevails between parents, the mother attempts to satisfy her thwarted need for affection by overindulging her son, especially the eldest one. She uses him as a means of annoying her husband. Consequently, violent antagonism develops between father and son, with the son openly blaming the father for the family troubles. The critical point is reached when the mother loses her nerve under severe strain and turns on the boy, accusing him of being the source of trouble.

7. **Mentally Ill Mother:** In a family where the mother is mentally ill and her mental disturbances have reached a stage where the strain of living

with her has become almost unbearable, the father will try his best to be away from home. He will find other sources of part-time recreation that will make his presence at home much shorter.

8. **Lack of Maternal Concern:** The mother's lack of concern for the child often results in the latter being left with the grandmother or some other woman. In such a scenario, the child will develop and express affection for the foster mother or its father.

9. **Father's Long Absence From Home:** When the father remains away from home due to some reason during the child's early years, it seems a form of emotional rejection for the child. This causes a disturbance in the child, which the father interprets as bad behaviour. He fears that other children will become affected with his child's crankiness. This attitude often causes quarrels between the parents, which may result in the mother herself turning against the child for the sake of "family unity".

   Threats to have the child put away in a hostel-like institution produce a counter-reaction of self-banishing hostility. The child resorts to creating a nuisance, running away and stealing within the home. Often, this situation is caused by the anxious-hostile personality of the father, but it can also arise in families of highly principled parents who take too serious a view of the child's lying and other misdemeanours.

10. **Mother Forced to Bear Undue Strain:** In some cases, the father exerts undue and excessive pressure on the mother, through sickness or an inability to work, through unbalanced behaviour

or by lack of support in running the family. Consequently, the mother faces a combination of mental stress, sheer physical overwork and an inability to manage her family, thereby reaching a stage of irritable, depressive non-tolerance. In this state, she reacts violently against any source of disturbance or annoyance. She may even temporarily express dislike for her child.

11. **Child's Preference for Grandmother:** In some homes, the child shows his preference for the grandmother rather than his mother. Because the grandmother shields the child from the mother's disciplinary nature, she is regarded as the epitome of kindness and all good things, while the child rejects the mother as she is the one who denies, disciplines and punishes. But later on, in the absence of the grandmother or another motherly figure, the child cannot easily reverse this attitude towards his real mother. In such a situation, unable to exercise any discipline, the real mother may allow herself to be dictated to by the child in a bid to regain her child's affection.

12. **Child Fearing Abandonment:** In some cases, the child fears he will be abandoned. This fear of abandonment may be due to adoption, remarrying of the mother after a divorce or death of the father. In such instances, the fear of abandonment may induce in the child an inhibition against any affectionate attachment and he may develop violent hostility.

OOO

3

Influence of the Environment on Children

Impact of Divorce on Children

Children who live with their divorced mothers, especially boys, face more social, academic and behavioural problems. A number of factors influence children's adjustment to the fallout of divorce and their adjustment with society. These include:

(a) **Parenting Style and Satisfaction:** Children of authoritative divorced parents show fewer problems at school and with other children. With those parents who are able to control their anger, children have fewer emotional and social problems.

(b) **Remarriage of the Mother:** Remarriage demands adjustment. Research studies have shown that remarried mothers tend to be happier, better adjusted and more satisfied with life. Their sons do better with the stepfather, but daughters have more problems than the daughters of divorced mothers who have not remarried.

(c) **Relationship with Father:** In adolescent boys whose parents had divorced ten years ago, the relationship with the father influences their post-divorce adjustment with the mother. The sons of erratic and rejecting fathers feel humiliated and hurt and often react with anger against their mothers.

(d) **Accessibility of Both Parents:** Predictable and frequent contact with the parent who is not easily accessible is most important. The typical practice of limited visitation for fathers deprives children of the desired love and protection. This acts like rejection.

Influence of the Employed Mother

Research studies have been undertaken to find out how the mother's employment influences the child's performance and personality. The findings show that the employed mother feels more competent, more economically secure and more in command of her children's lives. Her self-esteem tends to be higher than that of unemployed mothers. She is more satisfied with life and more effective as a parent.

In a family where the mother is working, the division of work is less traditional. The father is more involved in the children's upbringing and household work than his counterpart in the families of non-working mothers. He is most involved when his wife has a full-time job and they have more than one child. The involved father shows nurturing by expressing love, helping children with their concerns and problems through care and attention. This is not the case with fathers in non-working mothers' families; with working mothers and involved fathers, children have fewer stereotypes about gender roles.

School-age children of employed women have two advantages over children of non-employed mothers. They tend to live in more structured homes with clear-cut rules and household responsibilities. They are more encouraged to be independent. This makes the children, especially daughters, feel more competent to achieve more in school and have higher self-esteem. Daughters of working mothers tend to be more independent and have a more positive attitude towards being a female than those of mothers who are at home.

Sibling's Influence

Siblings influence each other directly through their interaction and indirectly through their impact on each other's relationship with the parents. Siblings' interaction with each other helps them develop self-confidence. Children learn a lot of new things from their brothers and/or sisters. They also learn to resolve conflicts. Though they may quarrel, they know that it will not mean the end of the relationship. Compromise, negotiations and being sensitive to the other's needs are skills they learn through conflicts.

First-borns tend to be dominating and the younger ones tend to be more skilful in resolving conflicts. Interdependence, caretaking and nurturing constitute other aspects of social skills that siblings learn through mutual interaction. Elder girls explain more to younger siblings than boys do. Older brothers tend to be more aggressive and bossy in their attitude.

Why Children like Comics

While reading comics, children find an escape from their real environment. The comic allows the child to identify himself with an all-powerful and always right hero. On reaching the last stage of childhood, the child is able to give up comics as his tastes and abilities mature.

However, it would not be correct to assume that maturity occurs only when comics have been given up. In many ways, comics reflect the changing times of our society. One can hardly assume that to continue reading comics is a hallmark of immaturity. Children ultimately find that comics do not meet their needs for aesthetically pleasing material. They also find that the material is highly unrealistic in relation to their everyday problems. At this time, they are ready to move towards more realistic stories or books.

Give him space of his own

For many children, comics become a "coin of the realm" – they can be bartered for marbles and other tokens of value for the child. As the child matures, the value of this material tends to diminish.

There is a body of evidence to reassure parents and teachers about the effects of comics upon school-going children. On comparing children who read a lot of comics with those who read them rarely, it was found that both groups had the same intelligence levels. Although individual reading patterns varied a great deal, some children classed as 'comic readers' had excellent overall reading programmes. There were no distinguishing characteristics that marked readers or non-readers of comics.

The child who feels a need to be delinquent, or to escape from the demands of life, appears to find comics useful. Comics seem to be the most readily obtainable means to help him achieve his end. When the child reads any comic, he is exposed to many new words that increase his vocabulary.

There are many reasons why comics appeal to children. They are readily available, inexpensive, rely on a simple and exciting story line and are profusely and colourfully illustrated. The print is generally large and the books are short. They become barter material, too.

Goal-directed Behaviour

Parents should always bear in mind that the behaviour of children is often goal directed and the result of a desire to satisfy needs. These needs are the result of the normal interaction that takes place between an individual and his environment. These needs do not evolve only in a person's mind, or result from the environment alone, their origin is a consequence of the environment-individual mix. Certain goals are highly positive, and the need for achieving them is high. Other goals are not positive. For example, because of peer pressure a child may have an intense desire to learn cycling, whereas he may not view book learning with the same degree of positiveness.

We often feel frustrated in achieving goals when the necessary repertoire of skills has not been developed. The main needs of the child are attention, affection, activity, acceptance and success. When one is thwarted in achieving a goal, he can either make another frontal attack, attempting to penetrate or circumvent the barriers or, after repeated failures, he can search for a reasonable substitute for the goals that he finds unattainable through direct means.

To reduce tension, an individual must either achieve his goal or engage in some type of socially accepted and situationally appropriate alternate behaviour.

INFANT'S EMOTIONS

Infants show their emotions in different ways. When an infant is uncomfortable, he cries, stiffens his body and flings his arms and legs around. When the baby is happy, he shows it through different expressions. During the first month when infants become quiet on hearing a human voice or when they are picked up, they smile. When their hands are moved together in play, they smile, coo, reach out and eventually move towards people. All these are signs and reliable clues of the baby's emotions.

When they need something, they cry; when they feel sociable, they laugh and smile. Their sense of personal power grows as they see that their cries bring help and comfort, and their smiles and laughter elicit a similar response from others. But these emotional expressions convey different meanings as the baby grows. At first, crying is a signal of physical discomfort; later on, it expresses psychological distress.

Here is a brief description of an infant's specific emotions:

Crying

There are four crying patterns: the basic hunger cry, the anger cry, the pain cry, and the frustration cry. The hunger cry is rhythmic, and the anger cry has a variation of rhythm. The pain cry is often sudden and loud, while the frustration cry is accompanied by two or three drawn-out cries without prolonged holding of the breath.

An infant's cry must be responded to with care and tenderness. If the mothers do so, their infants cry less by the time they are a year old, compared to those whose cries were not responded to quickly by their mothers.

Smiling

The first smile occurs soon after birth, as a result of central nervous system (CNS) activity, often when the baby is asleep. In the second week, babies often smile after getting their feed. When they are drowsy they may be responding to the caregiver's sounds. Later, smiles come more often when the babies are alert but inactive.

After about one month, the baby's smiles become frequent and more social. They smile when their hands are clapped together or when they hear a familiar voice. During the second month, they become more receptive to people whom they already know.

Laughter

Babies start laughing around the fourth month. Some of their laughter may be related to fear because sometimes they react with the same stimulus to both fear and laughter. As they grow older, they respond to sounds and cough and may be delighted by games at seven to nine months. This shift reflects cognitive development. Laughter is a response to the environment, which helps babies discharge tension in situations that otherwise might be upsetting. Laughter represents an important relationship between cognitive development and emotional development.

EFFECTS OF TV ON CHILDREN'S BEHAVIOUR

Some time or the other everyone shows aggression in a way that brings discomfort to others. The type of aggression that a person displays and his ability to control such actions change significantly with age and experience.

Many parents feel that their children are more likely to become aggressive when they are upset, agitated or excited. Research has shown that emotional arousal does appear to influence a child's willingness to become aggressive and that the process may operate differently in boys and girls. Overall, the level of aggression is more in boys than in girls.

Excessive viewing of violence on television could
make your child aggressive

Although children may be provoked into aggression by irritating or provoking events in their environment, most aggressive acts also have a basis in the child's past learning history. Youngsters usually follow aggressive behaviour or those who have come across a number of aggressive models are prone to learn aggressive behaviour that can be easily activated whenever provocations occur. Children can also learn ways of behaving aggressively by merely watching others indulging in such behaviour, no matter that the aggressive model is punished for such hostile behaviour.

The same principles apply to the television model of aggression. Therefore, serious questions have been raised about the portrayal of violence in children's television programmes. Youngsters could learn novel aggressive responses from television and television-like formats. Research findings show that the more the child watches violence on TV, the more aggressive he is likely to be.

Findings of UNESCO Study

According to a report published in *The Hindustan Times*, a survey was conducted in 2000 about acts of violence aired on TV. After studying five channels for nine days through 759 acts of telly violence, Zee topped the chart and Doordarshan had the least telly violence.

Zee TV's 'scorecard' had registered 365 points against DD's 62. Star TV was number two with a score of 188 and Sony had 64 points. Interestingly, DD II's violence ratings at 80 were higher than Sony's.

According to a study conducted by UNESCO, *X-Zone* and *Anhonee* on Zee were found to have a higher degree of violence, compared to *Kohra* on Star Plus and *Aahat* on Sony.

Making a clear distinction between audio and visual violence, the study categorised eerie soundtrack and threatening music to be audio violence against visual violence that included shooting, assaulting and stabbing, amongst other acts of violence. In addition to the excessive depiction of murder, bombing and burning, many serials depict verbal abuse, bizarre sound effects and, occasionally, psychological violence.

Even when care was taken to avoid acts of physical violence, certain serials repeatedly used hallucinations, nightmares and paranoia for an effective build up of an atmosphere of terror, the study noted.

Yet, more than the violent content, what was really disturbing was the trend of horror shows and crime serials to target the child viewer. Surveys indicate that children eagerly watch many of these programmes.

Adjustive Mechanisms to Release Tension

Each of us has a certain moment by moment tolerance level against frustration and tension. When this level is reached or exceeded, there is a need for tension to be released through some type of adjustive or defensive behaviour. Then, the choice before an individual is to use any type of behaviour to protect his integrity, if he fails to achieve his goal and feels frustrated.

Behaviours such as classified aggression, substitution, withdrawal, projection, suppression and reaction formation come under the category of adjustive mechanisms, when people choose to relieve their tension.

These mechanisms are defined below:

Aggression : Behaviour aimed at hurting someone or destroying something.

Substitution : Acceptance or satisfaction with substitute goals in place of those originally sought or desired.

Withdrawal : Intellectual, emotional or physical retreat.

Projection : Ego-defence mechanism in which individual attributes his own unacceptable desires and impulses to others.

Suppression : Conscious inhibition of desire or impulses.

Reaction Formation : Ego-defence mechanism in which individual's conscious attitudes and overt behaviour are the opposite of his repressed subconscious wishes.

We know that an individual's view of his own capabilities and level of achievement is based to a large degree on his history of success and failure within a given environment.

For example, if a child has not had an opportunity to succeed in school activities and constantly failed, he will develop a complex network of antagonisms towards those activities. This may result in the youngster eventually exhibiting a general dislike for anything associated with school. He will begin to view himself as inadequate and may even develop a dislike for or become hostile towards authority figures, such as teachers.

OOO

4

Ways to Improve Children

BEHAVIOUR MODIFICATION TECHNIQUES

These techniques deal primarily with how to change overt student behaviour. This involves application of operant learning principles to bring about a specific change in behaviour.

The operant conditioning aims at getting a desired response from the person on whom it is being applied. Once the desired response occurs, it is reinforced to increase the frequency of its occurrence. This conditioning is also called instrumental conditioning.

Although behaviour modification originated as a technique based on operant conditioning, combinations of behavioural and cognitive approach are now the commonly used methods to bring about behavioural change. Operant conditioning methods use schedules of reinforcement and shaping to gradually achieve a desired response. Special prompts may be employed to highlight a situation that calls for a particular response.

Positive reinforcers such as praise and money are used to strengthen the desired responses. Token economies are special systems based on reinforcement principles, although they have not been as successful in raising the academic levels as they are reported to be in controlling social behaviour. In a token system, a unit of exchange (gift voucher, coupon, IOU slip, credit voucher and so on) is delivered contingent on a specified response. The token acquires the properties of a conditioned reinforcer, which can later be exchanged for a backup reinforcer, usually selected from various items, since in children what constitutes a reinforcer is idiosyncratic. Token reinforcement contingent on academic behaviour has been successfully used to improve academic performance.

Extinction procedure and punishment might be used to eliminate undesirable responses. When punishment is employed to eliminate a response, it is a good idea to simultaneously reinforce an alternative, more desirable, positive response. When no longer needed, gradual elimination of these unwanted behaviours is called fading.

Play and Family Therapy

Play Therapy and Family Therapy are two general methods of treating childhood problems. Generally, children are more reluctant than older people to voice their concerns and complaints directly and openly.

It is assumed that in play therapy a child will express his or her feelings about problems, parents, teachers and peers. This helps the adult therapist establish rapport with a youngster. A play-therapy room is equipped with puppets, blocks, games, puzzles, drawing materials, paints, water, sand, clay, toy guns, soldiers and a large inflated rubber clown to punch. These toys help children vent their inner tension and concerns.

Children usually live with parents and siblings, with whom their lives are inextricably linked. Therefore, therapists examine and attempt to alter the pattern of interaction in families, rather than treating the troubled child or young adolescent alone.

The child's problem has been caused or is sustained by disturbed relationships within the family. For example, the father may have abdicated his responsibilities.

The Importance of Token Economies

Approval and other intangible reinforcers often prove ineffective in behaviour therapy, especially ones dealing with severely maladaptive behaviour. In such instances, appropriate behaviours may be rewarded with tangible reinforcers in the form of tokens that can later be exchanged for desired objects or privileges.

The rules of the token economy are carefully framed and explained to the child. These clearly state the medium of exchange; the small routine tasks like eating, self-care etc. to be rewarded and by what number of tokens; the items and privileges that can be purchased, and for how many tokens.

The number of tokens earned by the child can be equated with the degree of desired behaviour that he manifests; the number of tokens earned and the way they are spent are largely up to the child. These tokens tend to bridge the gap between the institutional environment and the demands and rewards encountered in the outside world.

The ultimate goal is not only to achieve the desired responses but to bring such responses to a level where their adaptive consequences will be reinforcing in their own right, thus enabling natural circumstances rather than artificial reward contingencies to maintain the desired behaviour.

The Child's Emotional Growth

Emotional development begins early in life and stems from the generalised, undifferentiated reactions of the infant to stimulating situations.

These situations differ from child to child but are usually related at first to his physical well-being. The generalised responses become more diversified and specific as the child learns to discriminate between experiences and situations that give him satisfaction and those that do not.

We generally find two types of emotional behaviour: the pleasant or integrative feelings, and the unpleasant or disintegrative feelings. Rage, fear, jealousy, and disgust are considered disintegrative feelings; joy, elation, affection, delight and hope are termed integrative feelings. Both types of behaviour vary in degree or amount of response according to the individual and the situation experienced. If either type of emotions were carried to such an extreme that it became the dominating response regardless of the stimulus, disorganisation of the individual would result. Society places a high premium on integrative responses and attempts are made to minimise disintegrative responses, except in isolated periods of environmental stress such as war, criminal action and so forth.

When the infant's physical needs are cared for, he is warm and satisfied. This feeling of well-being is first associated with the acts that produce the feeling and subsequently with the people performing the acts. As the child matures, he discovers ways of causing the pleasant action to occur. When he succeeds, his basic sense of trust is enhanced. When events do not happen as his experiences have taught him to expect, he becomes confused and uncertain about his environment and also about his own responses. Thus he develops a pattern of response that works in most situations to obtain the desired result. When he is unsuccessful in coping with a particular situation, or when he has no preconceived response, unpleasant emotions such as fear and anger follow, contributing to the feeling of distrust.

As children gain in intellectual abilities, in physical and motor skills, and in awareness of the significance of their environment, they acquire emotional reactions and patterns appropriate to their level of development and their experiences. The four-year-old child tends to be afraid of the dark, goblins and ghosts, while the 12-year-old is afraid of such things like school failure, tardiness and not being liked by others.

Under essentially the same conditions, two children will react quite differently due to their emotional growth. For example, one child expresses joy and pleasure at being able to hold a kitten, while another moves back in fear and refuses any physical contact with it.

Some investigators have claimed that emotion is hereditary and instinctual; others feel that it begins as a physiological reaction; still others emphasise the environment as the source of differentiated emotional response.

When children engage in actions that are not easily understood, that are less common and more surprising, we call them emotionally disturbed children.

The Importance of Motor Development

The development of motor skills is essential for participation in group activities during childhood. Many informal social contacts centre on the performance of motor activities. The child who does not achieve proficiency in skills like cycling, ball playing, skipping and gymnastics is likely to be left on the fringe of group activities.

Successful learning of motor skills has an effect on personality development. Children gain personal satisfaction and a feeling of achievement from well-executed physical activities and the ability to compete successfully with others. Motor achievement leads to social status among peers and greater group acceptance.

Good motor skills aid personality development

Before skills can be learned the child must be mature. Once maturation is reached, the opportunity to practise and the attitudes of the people with whom the child associates are important factors in determining the degree of skill acquired. Parents can encourage children to learn by showing interest in and enthusiasm about his performance. While it may be necessary to set physical limits for the safety of the child, an overprotective attitude or undue concern may discourage his initiative and interest in motor activities.

Equipment that encourages practice in both gross and fine body movements should be made available to children. Between the ages of five and eight, most children need experience in the use of large muscles. Running, climbing and jumping games are not only popular but also foster co-ordination and efficiency of movement.

Opportunities to practise fine motor skills, such as hammering, sawing, drawing and cutting with scissors, are also important. But these activities require more refined coordination and will be performed more skilfully by 10- and 11-year-olds. Young children are more interested in learning how to use the tools than in the finished product.

Teaching Social and Personal Skills

Behaviour is the result of a person's interaction with his environment. Repeated behaviour of the same type occurs because of the individual's expectation that the environment will in some way reinforce the behaviour that is of value to him.

While studying this complex process, psychologists have attempted to alter, manipulate or control the environment in various ways in an effort to modify an individual's behaviour. The term *behaviour modification* has been used to describe this approach.

A child's behaviour is changed by consequent parental reaction to it. If you provide a child with something he wants after he has behaved in a certain way, that behaviour will increase. If you withhold the reinforcer, the behaviour will eventually disappear. If you punish the child, the undesired behaviour will decrease immediately but will probably recur soon.

The immediacy with which the reinforcer is applied and the degree to which you are consistent with the consequence are both important considerations. After a behaviour has become established, it can be maintained by reinforcing once in a while or adopting a gambling schedule where the child never knows when he will receive the reinforcer and so tries harder and longer in anticipation of the reward.

You must also be careful not to expect too much from a child at the very beginning. Otherwise, you would end up never reinforcing him because he could not reach a higher goal set by you.

Remember – reinforce successive approximations to the goal but never reward the child when he returns to the level of performance he had already attained. Caution should be exercised so that undesirable behaviour is not rewarded. This occurs frequently, particularly in cases involving discipline. Many children seek attention by misbehaving all too frequently. Teachers as well as parents reward misbehaviour by calling attention to it. And, children seeking attention are reinforced in this behaviour. In most instances, the preferred technique for handling a social or behaviour problem is to ignore the person misbehaving. Certain reprehensible circumstances require that the child be removed from the environment or administered some type of punishment. Attempts should always be made to remove the possibility of the child being rewarded for misbehaviour.

In their efforts to help children understand and develop satisfactory social, personal and emotional behaviour, parents and teachers often lecture children about how and why they are to behave in a certain fashion. Even with the best of intentions, this method of instruction will have only minimal impact for several reasons. First, lecturing assumes that the children have developed language and conceptual skills needed to understand abstract notions. Secondly, lecturing is a poor strategy since it does not provide the children opportunities to look at themselves and evaluate their own performance. Each child must be given opportunities to engage in activities that will help him evaluate the reasons for and against behaving in a certain fashion under various circumstances.

An acceptable pattern of behaviour will be most

rapidly and effectively acquired under the dual influence of models and differential reinforcement. Children will value and reflect the behaviour of models they consider to be of high credibility. Moreover, they will react more favourably to the reinforcement provided by these "high-credibility" individuals than to those dispensed by a "low-credibility person".

Parents will find that the behaviour of children can be dramatically changed and subsequently controlled when models are used in ways that allow for imitation by youngsters.

Role of Punishment

Most parents perceive punishment as an effective corrective measure against their children's undesirable behaviour. All parents use it occasionally. But parents should bear in mind that, in comparison with punishment, reinforcement is most effective in building new patterns of behaviour.

The effects of punishment are suppressive. When punishment works, it reduces the likelihood of certain noxious or potentially dangerous responses. Punishment should always be administered in ways that have some significance for the child.

Time is very important in the naturalistic use of punishment against the young child. Acting in an extremely antisocial way, if a child hits a younger sibling, steals, resorts to lying or commits an act of vandalism, some time will inevitably pass before the transgression is detected. Even after detection, an extended waiting period may be present before potential punishment, as is evident in the familiar warning, *Wait till your father comes home.* It is therefore important to determine the relationship between the timing of punishment and its effectiveness.

As a rule, mild punishment will be maximally effective

if it is meted out immediately after the deviant act or while the act is occurring.

Remember that the punishment will be much less effective if its application is considerably delayed after the occurrence of the deviant act. Delayed punishment will be confusing in its purpose, at least for very young children.

If parents punish their child in the evening for a transgression committed in the morning, a situation may be created in which the child may show negative consequences after his desirable behaviour which the parents otherwise would have wished to encourage and reinforce.

Explain the reason for punishment to increase effectiveness

Punishment from a parent who is usually rewarding and nurturing towards the child is likely to be more effective than the same punishment from one who is usually cold and distant. Adults who practise what they preach are likely to be more effective in their reprimands than those who do not. Parents who follow punishment with a display of affection towards the errant children may counteract the impact of the punishment and will probably strengthen the undesirable response.

When punishment is used, it is desirable that the

child learns another response to substitute the one for which he was punished. For example, if a child fights frequently, his tendency to fight should be reduced and get substituted after punishment.

Explaining the reason for punishment increases its effectiveness. Reasoning and explanation play a very important role in the development of self-control among older children. These help children evaluate their own behaviour by explaining exactly what activity should be avoided and why.

Fostering Creativity

Training fosters creativity. It is possible to train a child to develop creativity. If freedom of exploration and decision is granted to a child, he starts moving towards creativity. The child should be suitably rewarded and encouraged for his new achievements. He should be allowed to develop without undue pressure. It should also be kept in mind that children with loving parents tend to accept parental attitudes and thus become somewhat conformist in nature. Parents who are unreasonable or too rigid, on the other hand, may encourage a rebellious attitude in their children that will lead to independent thinking and action.

Always remember that rewards can play a vital role in developing many aspects of behaviour. Incentives can increase children's creativity. But in all likelihood such training will produce only moderate changes in their creative performance.

The main components of creativity are: cognition involving discovery, awareness, recognition, comprehension or understanding; memory, involving retention and storage of information; divergent thinking, which involves the generation of information from the given information; convergent thinking, where the emphasis is on the use of the given information to produce the best response; and evaluation, or reaching decisions or making judgements concerning the correctness, suitability, adequacy, and desirability of information in terms of criteria of identity, consistency, and goal satisfaction.

OOO

SELF-IMPROVEMENT/PERSONALITY DEVELOPMENT

Also Available in Hindi

Also Available in Hindi

Also Available in Kannada, Tamil

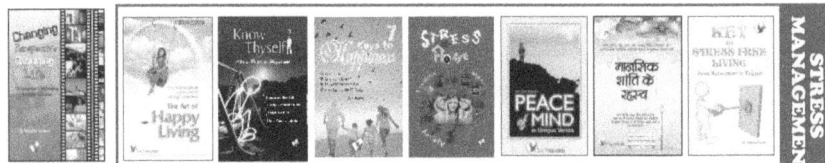

Also Available in Kannada

Also Available in Kannada

STRESS MANAGEMENT

All books available at www.vspublishers.com

www.ingramcontent.com/pod-product-compliance
Lightning Source LLC
Chambersburg PA
CBHW061756040426
42447CB00011B/2328